THE LETTER E

HAVAH FLEISNER & TRACY WELAK

ART BY MIKE COLLER

Zack's Book Shack

Est. 1974

WHILDEN PUBLISHING

ISBN: 979-8-9953996-0-5 Hardback
ISBN: 979-8-9953996-1-2 Paperback
ISBN: 979-8-9953996-3-6 Digital online
ISBN: 979-8-9953996-2-9 Hardback - Large Print Edition
Published by: Whilden Publishing
Children's Imprint: Zack's Book Shack

This is a work of fiction inspired by real-life experiences. Names, characters, places, and incidents are either products of the author's imagination or used with permission.

For information, contact:
Whilden Publishing

Printed in the United States of America

We dedicate this book to **God**,
the Author of our story,
who fills our lives with courage, hope,
and endless love,
and reminds our family that even without
perfect sight, our story is still
beautifully written.

With all our love,

Tracy and Havah

JOHN 8:12

When Jesus spoke again to the people, he said, "I am the light of the world. Whoever follows me will never walk in darkness, but will have the light of life."

Stargardt Macular Degeneration

Grace is legally blind because of Stargardt Macular Degeneration. This means her vision is limited.

The center of her vision is blurry, so reading small letters or seeing faraway can be tricky.

But Grace can still see through the outer part of her vision, called peripheral vision.

She notices movement and the world happening all around her.

Stargardt disease is genetic, which means it can be passed down in families.

Grace didn't know until she was 9 years old, when her vision began to change.

Sometimes, families carry these genes quietly and unseen until one day everything begins to make sense.

That is how Grace and her siblings, Waylan and Rose came to share this journey.

A Glimpse Through Grace's Eyes

"Look at my new glasses!"

Waylan shouted as he and Kip ran toward me.

He held them out proudly.

"Aren't they cool?"

“Not fair!” I groaned.

“I want an eye exam too!

I want my own blue pair!”

Mom called from
the kitchen,

"Grace, are you ready for

basketball practice?"

"I'm coming!" I grabbed my bag and hurried to the door.

I love basketball, but it has been really hard lately.

I stood with my hands up.

Wide open. Ready.

They looked... but didn't pass.

Maybe they don't think I am good enough. Maybe I really do need glasses like Waylan.

After begging Mom for weeks I finally sat in the big chair for my very first eye exam.

Kip sat on my lap, warm and calm.
I took a deep breath.

"E!" I said proudly.

"Good," the eye doctor said.

"Now the next line."

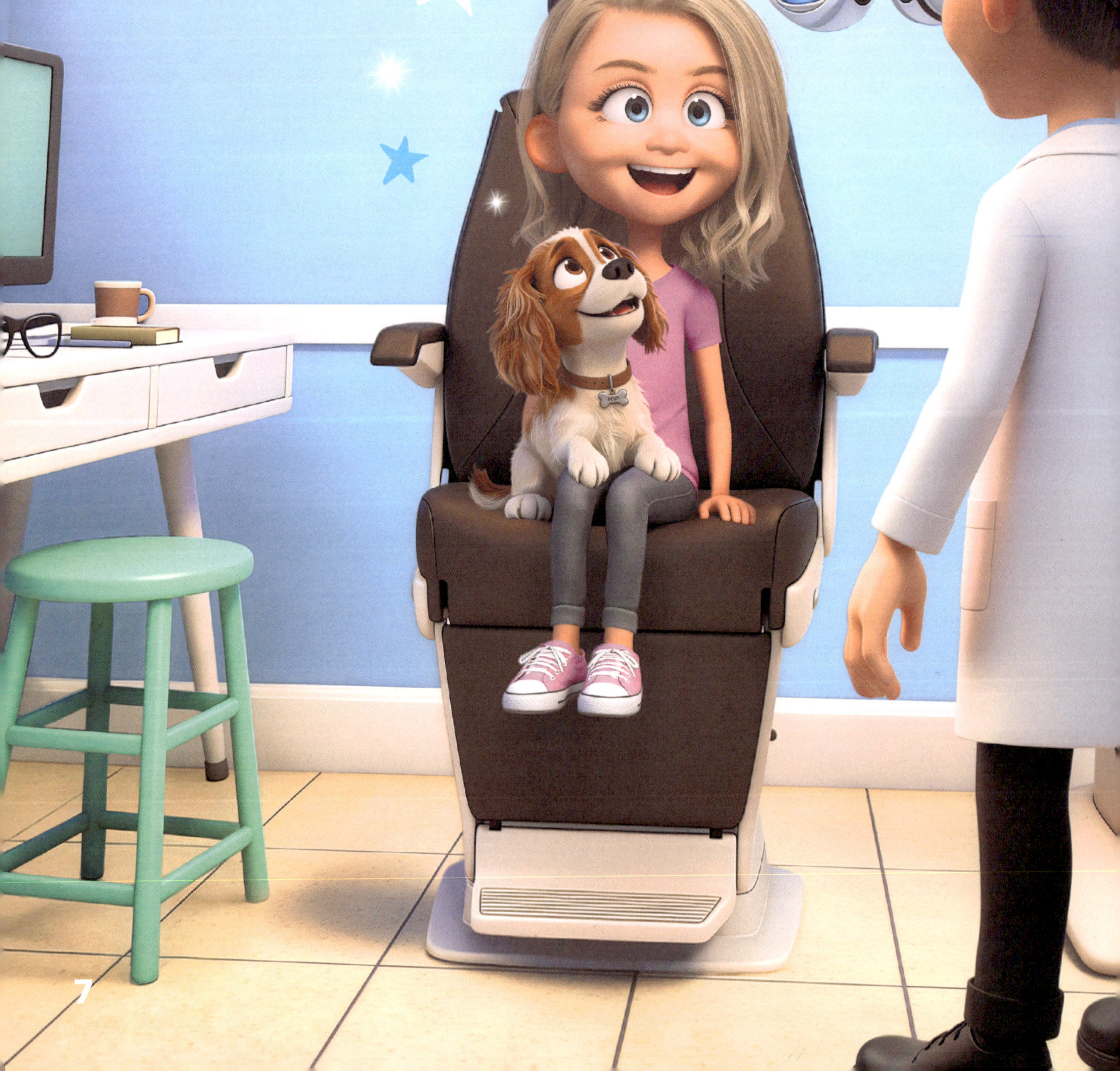

I squinted.
The letters blurred together.

My heart started beating faster.
My tummy felt funny, like something wasn't right.

"I can't see any more letters."

All I could see was the letter E.

I was still able to get my blue
glasses that day,
but they didn't help.

The ball still zipped past my hands
again and again. I tried my hardest.

I just couldn't catch the ball.

My coach pulled Mom aside,
his voice careful.
“Something isn’t right,” he said quietly.
“She’s not catching the ball.”
Mom looked worried.

Something was wrong.
But we didn't understand what.
Were my new glasses not strong enough?

We went to a new Doctor, hoping for answers.

Then another.

E...the Letter E!

What else is there to see!

"Kippy...I'm scared," I whispered to my best friend.

One doctor said I wasn't trying hard enough.

The other said I needed to talk to someone because I was lying.

But I wasn't lying. God tells us to be truthful, and I try every day to obey Him.

Mom knew I wasn't lying, so she took me to a new eye doctor. She carefully explained all the little signs she had been noticing over time.

I watched TV only inches away, held books almost to my nose, and during basketball, the ball kept flying past me. Things so simple felt so hard for me.

The doctor listened carefully.

Then she smiled softly saying, "I have an idea."

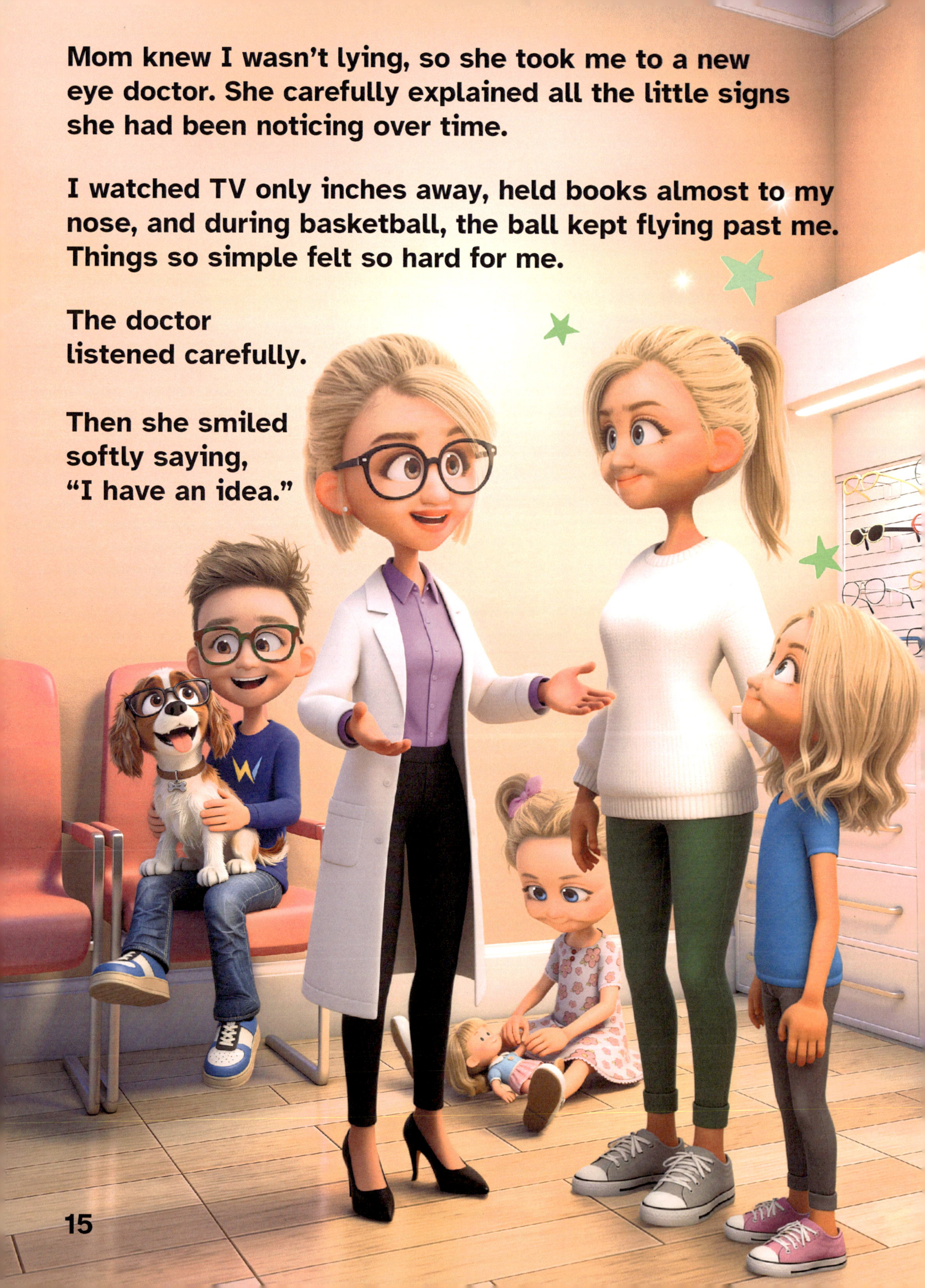

The doctor took pictures of my eyes with a special camera. I thought everything would finally be ok.

When she saw the results, she looked concerned.

She explained that she had seen something and that we needed to see a retina specialist.

Another office. Another appointment.

They were kind and gentle, and they saw the same thing. But this time, they knew exactly who we needed to see.

“One more doctor, Grace.” Mom looked just as tired as I felt.

Eye Health
EYE SCREENING
OUR FOCUS IS YOUR CLARITY

After a long day at a special eye clinic filled with more eye chart exams, pictures, bright lights, and eye drops, the nurse handed me a small tube.

"Spit in this," she said.

"Why would I need to spit in a tube?"

She said, "It's for genetic testing."

That's when we finally heard the truth.

"You have something called Stargardt macular degeneration," she explained gently.

"It's a genetic eye condition. It means the center of your vision is blurry, so your eyes use your peripheral vision to see the world."

She paused,

"You will never be able to drive."

"You are legally blind, Grace."

Mom explained that my eyes work better when
I look from the side instead of straight on.
My eyes leave out pieces of the world.
She said, "God made your eyes to see the world in
their own way, not like everyone else's."

And somehow,
that truth didn't feel heavy...
it felt gentle.

Mom said,
"You will still do great things.
God doesn't make mistakes.
You are beautifully made,
Grace."

Because Stargardt disease is genetic, it can be shared between family members.

That meant
Rose and Waylan
needed their eyes
checked too.

That was the day we
learned something big.

Mom tenderly explained to us
that we see the world the same way.
We all had Stargardt macular degeneration.

“We can be brave together,”
I said softly, trying to be strong for them.

"Pretty purple stars!
I am happy you're feeling safe again,"
Rose said softly.

"You can see how I've been feeling?"

Waylan said, “Of course, Grace... don’t you?”

The glimmer of stars were all around us.

“I see them,” I whispered. “I see all of them.”

Was this what it meant to see the world differently?

Just us, three siblings who had finally discovered we were seeing the same stars.

I knew then that God had given us the gift of seeing stars to help guide us and help us understand others more deeply.

Basketball felt different after that.
Defense became my strength.

I began to trust the sight I have and learned to move with what I could see.

When the point guard tried to get past me, I slid right into place without even thinking, my body moving with a confidence I hadn't felt before.

"Grace!" the coach called out.

"That's the best defense I've seen all season!"

"Grace," my teammate said, "We're going to pass you the ball. We want to help you make your first basket. Be ready to catch it."

"I'll be ready!"

I felt like I belonged on the team.

My teammate tossed me the ball.

I caught it and took the shot.
A defender jumped in front of me.

SMACK!

She blocked my shot and fouled me.

The whistle blew. My heart pounded. The referee pointed. "Free throw."

The ball felt heavy in my hands. I bent my knees, took a breath, and shot the ball.

SWOOSH!

The ball went in!

I scored my VERY first point!

We WON!

BLUE JAYS
5
BLUE JAYS
1
11

I felt bravery growing within me.

A quiet strength.

This is how I was meant to see the world.

I trust that God
will always
help us find our way.

With the stars softly
guiding us
I could face the world...
Through Her Eyes.

Star Feelings Chart

ABOUT the AUTHORS

Havah Fleisner and her mother, **Tracy Welak**, live in Wisconsin, where their family story inspires others through challenges, faith, and triumph. Havah, the oldest of three siblings, was diagnosed with Stargardt macular degeneration at age nine, shortly before her brother and sister received the same diagnosis. Living with visual impairment has shaped her perspective on resilience, courage, and the importance of family.

Havah is the founder of the *Through Her Eyes campaign* and has served as a public speaker for the blind and low-vision community through many foundations and opportunities. She encourages others with disabilities to embrace their potential. She loves audiobooks, singing, travel, and spending time with her beloved Cavalier King Charles Spaniel, Kip.

Tracy leads a busy life filled with love, faith, and dedication, guiding her children while supporting their dreams. She has found healing and joy in sharing their journey through writing, crafting a story inspired by true events to uplift and empower others. Tracy enjoys reading, learning, cooking, and celebrating life grounded in family and purpose.

LEARN MORE

Through Her Eyes - Living Life Legally Blind

@throughhereyescampaign_havah

TikTok @Through_Her_Eyes3

www.throughhereyescampaign.com

THROUGH Her EYES
Living Life Legally Blind

www.ingramcontent.com/pod-product-compliance
Ingram Content Group UK Ltd.
Pitfield, Milton Keynes, MK11 3LW, UK
UKRC031011310726
14089UKWH00015B/253

9798995399605

9 798995 399605